How Fragrant The Rose

Samplers and Historic Embroideries

1650 - 1850

EXHIBITION AT

Witney Antiques

96-100 Corn Street, Witney, Oxon OX8 7BU   Tel: 01993 703902   Fax: 01993 779852

Acknowledgements

Witney Antiques would like to thank the following individuals and societies for their help in providing original research which has gone into producing this our sixth catalogue.
Mr Phillip Joyce (catalogue entry No.7)
Mr Stephen Williams (catalogue No. 20)
The Society of Licensed Victuallers (catalogue entry No. 41)

Photography: Stephen Jarrett, Justin Jarrett

Catalogue Research and Text: Joy Jarrett, Rebecca Scott.

© Witney Antiques, 1998
Published by Witney Antiques
96-100 Corn Street, Witney, Oxfordshire OX8 7BU
Tel: 01993 703902 Fax: 01993 779852

Due to the printing process colours may vary slightly to those of the original samplers.

All rights reserved. No part of this publication may be reproduced, stored in a retrieval system, or transmitted, in any form or by any means, electronic, mechanical, photocopying, recording or otherwise, without the prior permission of the copyright holder.

ISBN 0 95181866X

Forward

The theme of our sixth annual exhibition of samplers and historic embroideries 'How Fragrant the Rose' is taken from a popular verse found on both British and American samplers.

'How fragrant the rose what a beautiful flower
The glory of April and May
But the leaves are beginning to fade in an hour
And they wither and die in a day.

Yet the rose has but one powerful virtue to last
Above all the flowers of the field
When its' leaves are all dead and the colours lost
Still, how sweet a perfume it yields'.

Rev. Isaac Watts. Moral Songs III. 'The Rose'

The English love of flowers is reflected in the outstanding embroideries which feature in this exhibition.
The rose, the emblem of England, multi-coloured pansies, honeysuckle, lilies, marigolds and cornflowers appear in many artistic variations, some worked with intense complexity, others the naive outgoing of an infant hand.

Included in the exhibition are some important and fine examples of spot motif, whitework and band samplers all dating from the mid 17th century and which we are proud to record.

As always on behalf of Witney Antiques we hope that all who have visited our exhibitions in the past, and this present one, will learn from it, and derive as much pleasure as ourselves from the wonderful legacy left to us from our forebears

1. Spot Motif Sampler. Circa 1650.

The 17th century is generally considered to be the 'golden age' of sampler making, and the two spot motif samplers (catalogue nos. 1 & 2) are amongst the rarest form of sampler worked at this period. Generally they are neither named or dated, being worked as a record of stitching techniques and individual motifs, both naturalistic and geometric in design.

Many patterns were copied or adapted from printed sheets available from book sellers, or were copied from 16th century woodcuts which illustrated the popular herbals of the day.

This rare spot motif sampler is a perfect example of it's type. Worked on linen in coloured silks and silver metallic threads, it comprises both naturalistic and geometric motifs worked in a wide variety of stitches.

The brilliant colours are as fresh today as when the sampler was originally embroidered.

Catalogue No 1 Spot Motif Sampler. Circa 1650

Unframed size: 9½" x 10½"
24cm x 27cm

2. Spot Motif Sampler. Circa 1650.

Worked on linen in coloured silks and silver metallic threads, this sampler comprises nine individual botanical motifs, six of which have braided metallic stems.

Five blocks of diaper patterns, a number of small insects and animals, and, as often found on this type of sampler, small individual patterns of metallic thread showing different stitching techniques.

Loan Exhibit.

Size: 9½" x 20"
24cm x 51cm.

Catalogue No 2:
Spot Motif Sampler.
Circa 1650

3. Whitework Sampler. Circa 1660.

A fine whitework sampler consisting of eleven bands of cut and drawn work with needle-lace filling stitches and pulled thread work, with geometric flower heads incorporated into the design.

Popular during the 17th century, whitework samplers generally show a high degree of skill, and to achieve the high standard with which they were worked needlework was begun at a very early age, and formed an important part of a young girl's education. During the 17th century girls were sometimes taught at school, but more usually at home by members of the household, or a governess.

Whitework or reticella samplers are generally composed of a series of border patterns which were of a type that could easily be incorporated into items of fashionable clothing, including sleeve frills, collars, coifs, christening robes and other items of domestic apparel.

Generally worked on loosely woven linen which was fairly easy to separate and count, the embroidery techniques include detached button-hole stitch, needlepoint, drawn and cut work. Bands of flower-heads figure prominently in most pieces.

Framed size: 9½" x 26"
24cm x 66cm

Catalogue No 3:
Whitework Sampler.
Circa 1660

4. Band Sampler. Circa 1660.

A magnificent mid 17th century band sampler, which employs a variety of stitching techniques, including six bands of whitework, with one band with the original vellum backing support. The method of working the design being clearly visible. Amongst the needle-lace designs employed are the Stuart S motif and stylised flower heads.

The top section, brilliantly coloured, displays a wide example of arcaded composite plants including roses, acorns and pansies. Another similar band consists of carnation heads.

To find such a sampler from this period in such fine condition and unfaded colour is indeed a rarity.

Unframed size: 7½" x 15½"
19cm x 39cm

Catalogue No 4:
Band Sampler.
Circa 1660

5. Band Sampler. Circa 1660. *HB*

This brightly coloured sampler bears the initials HB. These have been placed at the top of the sampler amongst a number of small geometric spot motifs.

Worked in silks on linen, the flat arcaded flowerheads of honeysuckle and roses form a contrast with the band of three dimensional stylised flowers, superbly worked in detached button-hole stitch.

A single boxer figure holding a flower between two plants is outlined in double running stitch, and presents a very clear example of this popular 17th century motif. Of all the motifs of this period the boxer and plant pattern is the one which probably excites the most curiosity.

The term 'boxer' derives from the figure's sideways stance, with one foot in front of the other and a raised arm with clenched fist, usually grasping a plant. They have been commonly identified as versions of Renaissance cupids or putti, whilst it has also been suggested that they might represent Daphne pursued by Apollo.*

* The Book of Samplers. Fawdry and Brown. Published 1980. Lutterworth Press. Page 42.

Size: 7" x 17½"
18cm x 45cm

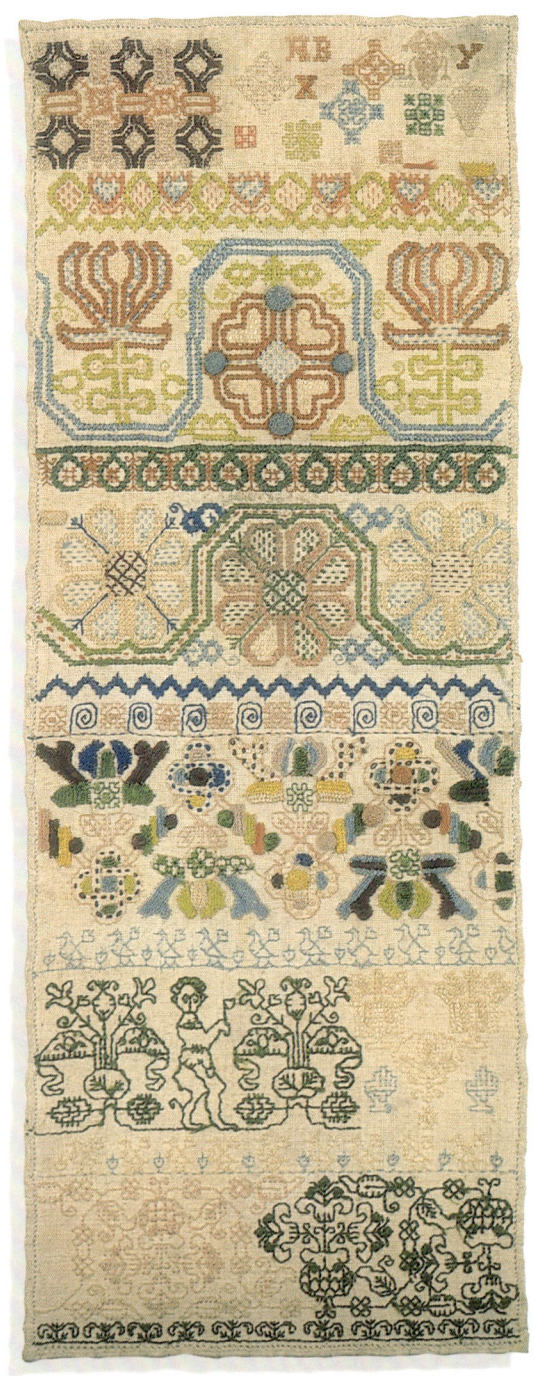

Catalogue No 5: Band Sampler. Circa 1660

6. Band Sampler. Circa 1660.

In common with many 17th century samplers this fine example bears neither a name or a date.

The most striking band of embroidery is pictorial and placed directly below four lines of alphabetical letters at the top of the sampler.

A fashionably dressed young woman, with corkscrew curls, the train of her gown held by a 'boxer' figure, stands beside a rose bush with perching birds.

The rose, worked in pink and white has been depicted, as is most common, full face. Chief amongst all flowers and occupying a foremost place on the coinage of the realm, it appears on most samplers worked at this period, along with the carnation, acorn, strawberry and 'boxer' figures.

Worked in coloured silks on linen.

Framed size: 10½" x 35"
26cm x 89cm

Catalogue No 6:
Band Sampler.
Circa 1660

Catalogue No 7: Band Sampler by Mary Molyneux. 1666

7. Mary Molyneux. 1666.

'I DID THIS WHEN I WAS NINE YEARS OF AGE. MARY MOLYNEUX 1666 SM.MM.'

This fine band sampler worked in coloured silks was completed in the year 1666, when on September 2nd much of London's medieval and tudor city was destroyed by fire. This included eighty-nine churches and the old gothic cathedral.

From genealogical research we believe that Mary came from a great and distinguished Norman family which at one time owned all the land upon which the city of Liverpool was built. The family were dedicated supporters of the crown and staunch Roman Catholics.

Her father, Sir John Molyneux, was born in 1623 and married Lucy Hesketh, the widow of Robert Hesketh. Lucy was the daughter of Alexander Rigby of Middleton, Lancs, who held the powerful position of Baron of the Exchequer.

Mary, born in 1657, was the eldest daughter from this union. At the age of twenty-three, in 1680, she married the Hon. Richard Leke. Their first and only surviving heir, succeeded as the Earl of Scarsdale.

Mary's step-brother from her mother's first marriage to Robert Hesketh, was Thomas Hesketh of Rufford Hall, who married Sidney, daughter of Sir Richard Grosvenor of Eton - ancestor to the present Dukes of Westminster. In turn Thomas's grand-daughter, Elizabeth married Sir Edward Stanley, afterwards 11th Earl of Derby.

The great Knowsley Estate at Prescot, Lancs. (Home of the Earls of Derby) adjoins the estate of the Molyneuxs (Earls of Sefton) at Croxteth.

In keeping with the political allegiance of the Molyneux family, the sampler indicates loyalty to the Stuart monarch by the presence of acorns and oak leaves as well as the Stuart S. The initials SM may in the catholic tradition be the first letters of the Latin for 'Holy Mother' ie. 'Mary, Mother of God', after whom Mary Molyneux, the eldest female child, would have been named. MM are her own initials.

A charming row of five boxer figures with raised needlepoint details, placed towards the bottom of the sampler, serve to emphasise Mary's skill with the needle.

Framed size: 36" x 13"
91cm x 33cm

8. Band Sampler. 1668. *SW*

Catalogue No 8: Band Sampler SW.
Dated 1668

This rare band sampler embroidered on linen in polychrome silks incorporates a number of complex stitches, including double running, satin, split, rococco, and detached button-hole etc.

The top band with a pair of royal figures, wearing crowns and probably representing Charles II and Catherine of Braganza. Dressed in fashionable clothes of the period, the collars on both costumes have been worked in detached button-hole stitch creating a three dimensional effect.

The two figures stand either side of a large urn-shaped vase, which amongst other flowers contains the ever popular tulip. First introduced into European gardens in the 16th century from Turkey, the tulip made a spectacular entry. It is said that in Holland single bulbs changed hands for fortunes.*

Below this pictorial section bands of stylised flowers delight the eye. These include the pansy, carnation, and tulip, worked in familiar undulating form.

Loyalty to the crown appears on the sampler in such motifs as the Stuart S, the rose and acorn. The latter firmly associated with Charles II, since his escape whilst trying to win back the English throne, by hiding in the branches of an oak tree at Boscobel House.

* The Embroiderer's Flowers. Thomasina Beck. Pub. David and Charles. 1992.

Framed size: 30½" x 10½"
77.5cm x 27cm

9. Katherine Carter. Circa 1670.

This very beautiful and complex band sampler worked in coloured silks bears the name of the embroideress above two rows of whitework.

The British love of flowers and the history of embroidery are fully intertwined in this outstanding sampler, which still retains much of its original vibrant colouring.

Worked in detached button-hole, three brilliant blue star-shaped cornflowers and a single multi-petalled deep pink rose with sprays of honeysuckle, form the widest and most distinctive band of flowers, forming a focus for the eye.

Below, various arcaded bands of stylised flowers, multi-coloured pansies, wild strawberries, acorns, and oakleaves form trailing vertical garlands.

Framed size: 9½" x 36½"
24cm x 93cm

Catalogue No 9: Band Sampler by Katherine Carter. Circa 1670

10. Unfinished Embroidery. 17th Century.

It is rare to have the opportunity to study an unfinished piece of embroidery of this period, in such pristine condition.

The designs for such embroideries were generally derived from wood-cuts, engravings or prints.

The method of transferring the design onto the silk or linen ground was quite simple. After tracing the design onto paper, the outline was transferred onto the ground fabric by perforating it with a needle, and rubbing charcoal or pounce (cuttlefish bone) through the holes. The design was then joined up with a solid line and sometimes shaded in.

The row of closely positioned black dots at the base of the small hillock, upon which a female figure sits, show us clearly that this was the method of transfer used.

The design is allegorical, representing the sense of smell. Twelve individual spot motifs of flowers surround a young woman who plays with her dog, and in one hand holds a tulip.

It is probable that the embroideress intended to stitch not only the individual motifs but also the background.

Size: 14" x 10½"
36cm x 26.5cm

Catalogue No 10: Unfinished 17th Century Embroidery

11. Martha Paston. 1737.

A small band sampler worked in coloured silks on linen. At this period the dominance of lettering prevailing over pattern bands, shows that literacy for young females was becoming increasingly important. Moral instruction could also be incorporated into the text.

'The heavens a book the stars are letters fair. God is the writer men the readers are. Children obey your......Lord for this is right. My......hear my voice and I know them so they follow me.'

Framed size 10" x 14"
25cm x 36cm.

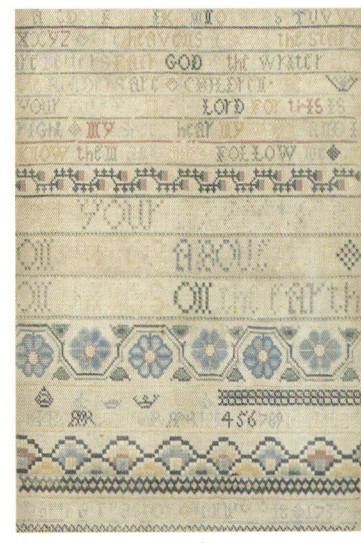

Catalogue No 11: Martha Paston. 1737.

12. Susanna Lombe. 1742.

Coloured silks on fine linen inscribed,'Susanna Lombe Wrought this Anno Dom 1742'

During the eighteen century the use of The Lord's Prayer on samplers became increasingly popular. The exquisitely worked border of scrolling flowers and leaves which encircle the central prayer have been painstakingly worked in the finest silks, delicately shaded using long and short stitch, with coiling stems supporting their colourful blooms.

Framed size: 12" x 15½"
31cm x 39.5cm

Catalogue No 12: Susanna Lombe. 1742

13: Polly Orchard. 1773.

This colourful, finely embroidered sampler worked in bright polychrome silks, shows a freestyle embroidery which became popular particularly during the latter half of the eighteenth century. The young Polly has combined the fashionable freely worked floral border with a nine line moral verse. Worked mainly in cross, satin, and stem stitch, and incorporating metallic threads, it makes an interesting comparison with the sampler (catalogue No. 14) by L. Langri∫h. Clearly both samplers have been worked under the direction of the same teacher. Private collection.

Framed Size: 22" 17½"
56cm x 44cm

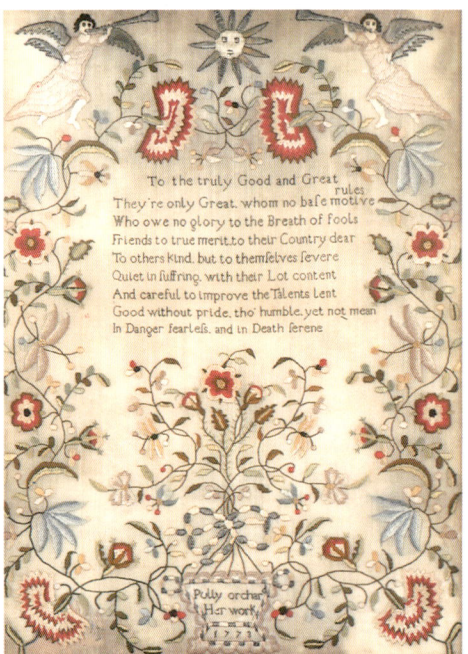

Catalogue No 13:
Polly Orchard. 1773.

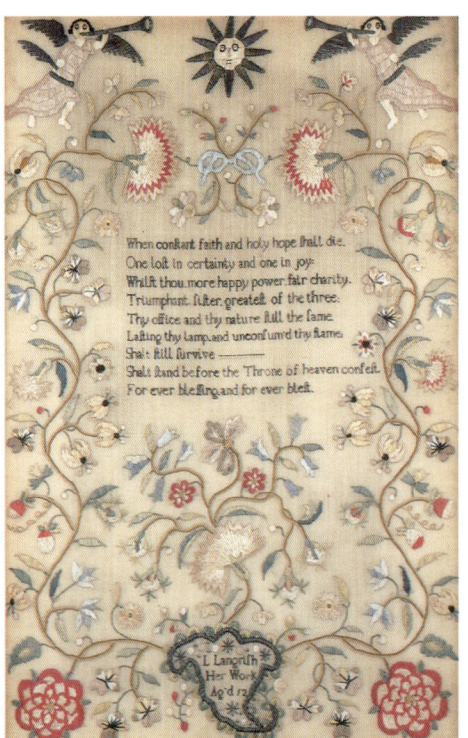

Catalogue No 14:
L Langri∫h. Aged 12. Circa 1773

14: L Langri∫h. Aged 12. Circa 1773

This sampler although undated is worked at approximately the same time as that by Polly Orchard. The colour choice, silks and metallic threads, stitching techniques, and format of the sampler clearly suggest the same teaching. With the principle difference being the choice of verse. During the eighteenth century the use of moral or religious verse on childrens samplers emerges. Books start to appear listing appropriate verses. The best known of these, first published in 1720, 'Divine and Moral Songs for Children' by Dr Watts, states that 'What is learned in verse is longer retained in memory and sooner recollected'. With so many ready made verses it is not surprising that the two girls chose to work different verses. Private collection

Framed size: 25" x 18"
63cm x 45cm

15. Tent Stitch. Mary Gail. 1788.

A charming tent stitched small picture, worked in wool and silk threads depicting a fashionably dressed couple.

The lady with a floral headdress and holding a flower, wears a pink striped robe which is open to reveal a blue striped petticoat. Her gentleman companion wears a blue frock-coat with deep cuffs. The couple stand, each with an arm outstretched towards the other, on flowery hillocks surrounded by fruiting stems and exotic blooms, including a deep blue cornflower and a pink dog-rose.

During the 17th century many embroideries were worked to commemorate a betrothal or marriage. It is fascinating to think that in common with this practice, Mary may also have worked this embroidery to commemorate her own marriage to 'WG'.

Framed size: 17" x15"
43.5cm x38cm

Catalogue No 15: Mary Gail. January 24 1788.

Detail of Catalogue No 15

16. 'Mary Blackxells Wrought this in the 15 year of her age 1791'.

The year in which Mary completed her charming sampler saw the first performance in Vienna of Mozart's opera 'The Magic Flute'. It was also the year in which Haydn composed his 'Surprise Symphony', and the waltz became fashionable in England.

A popular sampler verse has been chosen which gives praise to Mary's parents, and also dedicates the sampler to her friends.

'By this you see
What care my parents took of me.'
'this Work in hand my friends
may have
When I am dead and laid
in grave.'

Embroidered in coloured silks on fine wool the sampler has a naive quality which is most appealing.

Adam and Eve are depicted on either side of the Tree of Knowledge, below a beautifully worked blue sky, from which the sun, moon and stars all shine.

Catalogue No 16: Mary Blackxell. 1791

A text from the Book of Genesis, Chapter I, Verse 16, is an appropriate choice.

'And God Made tWo great light
the greater light to rule the day
and the lesser light to rule the night
he also made the stars.'

Bowls of freely worked flowers add to the exuberance of the sampler.

Framed size: 18½" x 18½"
47cm x 47cm

17. 'Fame Adorning Shakespeare's Tomb'. Late 18th century.

Many silk pictures, popular during the late 18th and early 19th centuries were based on paintings and engravings of the period. The working of them became regarded as a social accomplishment amongst young women of the leisured class.

They were originally bought, ready drawn on silk grounds, with the details such as the faces, arms, and the sky painted in. Generally the quality of the painting is very high, suggesting that they are the work of professional artists, and occasionally they bear the signature of the painter.

Amongst the most popular subjects embroidered are 'Fame Adorning Shakespeare's Tomb', also known by the alternative name 'Scattering Flowers over Shakespeare's Tomb' (1). The engraved source for this subject is a print by Bartolozzi after a drawing by Angelica Kaufman, and published by A Paggi in August 1782 (2).

Catalogue No 17:
'Fame Adorning Shakespeare's Tomb'

This beautifully embroidered version has been worked in long and short, satin and tiny running stitch onto a silk ground.

Other examples are in the following collections:

Victoria and Albert Museum, London.

Lady Lever Art Gallery. Liverpool.

Leicestershire Museums Service. Exhibition 1988 at the Whitworth Art Gallery, Manchester. 'The Subversive Stitch: Embroidery in Womens Lives. 1300 - 1900.' Cat. no 75 as 'Lady Scattering Flowers on a Tomb.'

(1) Bartolozzi and his Pupils in England. Selwyn Brinton. Pub. 1903. Page 33.

(2) Catalogue of Embroideries. Lady Lever Art Gallery. Xanthe Brooke. Pub. 1992.

18. S. Kemp. 1795.

Worked in coloured silks on muslin. This sampler uses simple darning techniques to create a garland of delicate multi-coloured flowers and leaves.

An ability to do such fine work would enable damask table linen and clothing to be repaired invisibly. Such skills would be a pre-requisite for the sought after position of ladies maid.

Framed size: 15½" x 15½"
39cm x 39cm

Catalogue No 18: Darning Sampler. S. Kemp. 1795.

19. Isabella Cooke. 1797.

This fine traditional and decorative darning sampler is subtly shaded in coloured silks on fine gauze and employs a number of different darning techniques. The central motif, a cornucopia of flowers, includes honeysuckle, the rose, and convolvulous. A meandering floral border of intertwining leaves and flowers forms the frame, with each large corner leaf spandrel worked with a different darning technique.
Framed size: 15" x 16"
38cm x 41cm.

Catalogue No 19: Darning Sampler. Isabella Cooke. 1797.

20. Ann Robinson. April 9, 1802.

Ann Robinson worked her sampler in the year that Sir Robert Peel introduced the 'Health and Morals of Apprentices Act' in Britain.

This act was introduced to protect young labourers in factories, many of whom worked in appalling conditions from dawn till dusk. Many of these children, as young as seven years old, were procured from the thousands of workhouses scattered throughout the country.

In contrast, Ann's sampler illustrates the comfort of the wealthy middleclass in Britain. Worked in expensive silks, and instructed by an accomplished teacher, Ann has achieved an exceptional standard of needlework. This may have been through the tutelage of a private governess or at one of the many small educational establishments that were springing up in every town in the country.

The broad arcaded band of roses, worked in lustrous floss silks,

Catalogue No 20: Ann Robinson. April 1802

draws the eye to the heart of the sampler. Delicately worked smaller motifs form an infil, whilst a moralistic verse provides the deemed appropriate tone. Probably Scottish.

Framed size: 16" x 18"
41cm x 46cm.

'Make much of precious Time while in your Pow'r
Be careful well to husband evry (sic) hour
For what shall come when you shall sore Lament
The unhappy Minutes that you have mispent'

21. Honora Teresa Mulligan. 1804.

This unusual oval sampler, worked in coloured silks on linen is set in the original verre Èglomisè mount with rosette spandrels, and the embroideresses name, HONORA (spelt Honoria on the sampler) TERESA MULLIGAN.

This form of mount, bearing a name, is not a common way of framing British samplers, but is seen more frequently on pieces from America.

The sampler is bordered by an attractive band of intertwined flowers knotted together by a bow, as are the flowers surrounding Honora's name and date of completion. The religious motif IHS and verse, along with her name suggest a strong Irish connection.

Framed size: 16½" x 23"
42cm x 59cm

Catalogue No 21:
Honora Teresa Mulligan. 1804

22. Elizabeth Stocking. Wells School. Circa 1805.

Catalogue No 23:
Elizabeth Stocking.
Circa 1805

Embroidered on fine muslin with coloured silks this delicate sampler is worked using a variety of stitches. The verse is contained within a meandering central oval of realistically and freely worked flowers. The stems of honeysuckle, roses, convolvulus and carnations all intertwining.

'Go rule thy will Bid thy wild pafsions all be still Know God and bring thy heart to know
The joys from which Religion flow
Then every grace shall prove it's guest And I'll be there to crown the rest.'

Although the sampler clearly states that it was worked at Wells School, we have been unable to ascertain in which town the school was situated. 'Taking the Waters' was considered health-giving at this time and spa towns flourished. (Wells in Somerset, Malvern Wells, Tunbridge Wells, Matlock etc). Hence in such localities the name Wells School would have been a popular choice.

Framed Size: 16½" x 20"
44cm x 51cm

23. Elizabeth Mary Bale. 1806.

In the year Elizabeth worked her sampler, Beethoven composed his popular Violin Concerto, Op. 61 and his Fourth Symphony No. 4 in B flat major.

Worked on a cream wool ground with coloured silks, a carefully charted design of a stag in a forest has been placed between two popular religious verses. Baskets of flowering roses, exotic birds and a pair of greyhounds complete the sampler, which is contained within an attractive geometric floral border of honeysuckle, strawberries and bell flowers.

PROVENANCE. Miss Carrie B Neely. Chicago. Collection Museum of Science and Industry, Chicago. 1939 - 1998.

Framed size: 22' x 24'
56cm x 61cm.

Catalogue No 23: Elizabeth Mary Bale. Clapham, Surrey. 1806

24. Janet Arneil. Port Glasgow. 1807.

Although Janet Arneil did not embroider her birthplace on her sampler the family surname provides the first clue to it's Scottish origin.

'JANET ARNEIL
SEWED THIS SAMPLER
IN THE YEAR 1807'

'Arneil' is a surname found in Glasgow and its environs and it is from this area of Scotland that the Arneil family came.

Glasgow, the third most populous city in Britain, grew at a phenomenal rate during the Industrial Revolution. Its commercial prosperity beginning in the 17th century when its merchants set out to dominate the trade of the western seas. New World produce, tobacco, sugar, and cotton poured into the wharf's newly built town of Port Glasgow, situated on the south bank of the Firth of Clyde estuary. Between these two centres lay the town of Renfrew and it was here at the parish church that Janet's father married Hellen Brown on Dec. 22, 1778.

During the next few years the Arneils and their growing family moved from Renfrew into the centre of Glasgow to the notorious Gorbals district.

In 1788 the 10th Earl of Eglinton built a new town on the outskirts of Glasgow, on the road between Kilmarnock and Hamilton, six miles south of the city. Cottages were built to house workers whom he employed in the silk weaving business. It was here in 1791 that Janet was christened in the new parish church.

It is possible that the family moved once more, this time to the silk weaving centre at Strathavon, for it is here at the village of Glassford, just two miles away that at the age of twenty-five Janet married Robert Hamilton.

Janet's sampler worked in coloured silks on fine wool was embroidered when she was sixteen years old.

Within the formal carnation border the main design of a large bouquet of flowers has been worked in long and short stitch. This was drawn free-hand as traces of the pencilled outline are visible. Other motifs include a broad arcaded floral band, small birds, trees and animals etc.

Framed size: 18" x 22"
46cm x 56cm

Catalogue No 24: Janet Arneil. Port Glasgow. 1807

25. Elizabeth Gill. 1809.

Worked on a cream wool ground in coloured silks, the sampler bears the text from 'LUTHER'S HYMN', beginning;

'GREAT GOD what do I see or hear......'

Contained within a stylised honeysuckle border, the verse is surrounded by mounds of fruit in bright scarlet and blue pots, small birds and flowers. The presence of four large thistle sprays to the corners may indicate a Scottish origin to the embroiderers background, along with the surname GILL, a name of great antiquity and with many variants common in Scotland.*

* 'Surnames of Scotland. Their Origin, Meaning and History.' George F Black. Pub Birlinn.
PROVENANCE. Miss Carrie B Neely. Chicago. Collection. Museum of Science and Industry. Chicago. 1939 - 1998.

Framed size: 19" x 21"
48cm x 53cm

Catalogue No 25: Elizabeth Gill. 1809

26. The Wish. Early 19th Century.

'You whose fond wishes do to Heaven aspire;
And make that Blest abode your sole desire.
If you be wise and hope that Bliss to gain;
Use well your time and use not an Hour in vain:
Let not the Morrow your vain thoughts employ;
But think this Day the last you shall enjoy.'

Sadly the young embroideress who stitched this delightful sampler chose neither to include her name, age or a date.

Worked on a cream wool ground in fine cross stitch with coloured silks, the sampler is composed of a popular verse and a number of individual spot motifs of birds, small animals and potted plants.

Framed size: 16" x 20"
41cm x 51cm

Catalogue No 26: The Wish. Early 19th Century

27. Mary Ann Mitchell. Circa 1810.

That Mary embroidered her exceptionally fine sampler at the age of ten years must bear tribute to both her skills with a needle and to a most talented teacher who instructed her in the art of embroidery.

Worked on a cream wool ground with brightly coloured silks, a multi-coloured floral border frames the sampler.

A short six line optimistic, religious verse occupies the top section which is separated by a band of carnations from a charming, rural scene depicting a picturesque cottage, willow trees and a grey horse.

A further band of flowers, stylised tulips and a wreath of flowers and leaves containing Mary's name and age complete the sampler.

PROVENANCE. Miss Carrie B Neely, Chicago. Collection. Museum of Science and Industry. Chicago. 1939 - 1998.

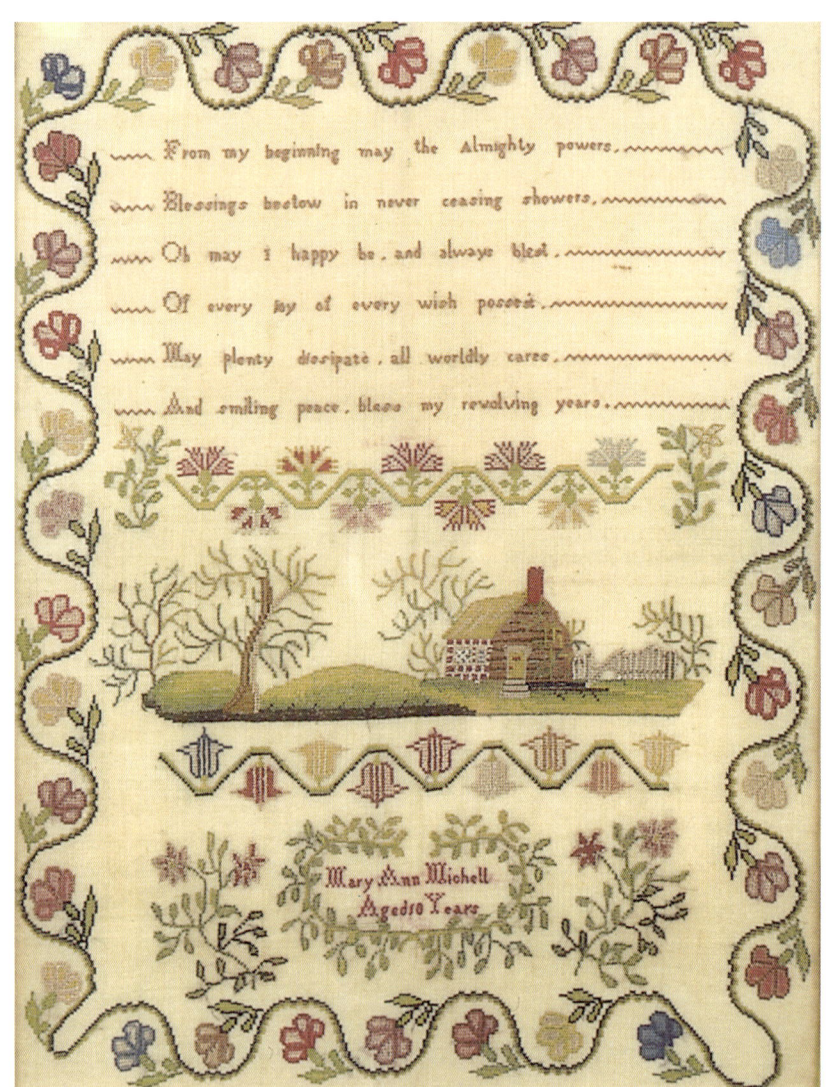

Catalogue No 27: Mary Ann Mitchell. Circa 1810

Framed size: 22½" x 19"
56cm x 47.5cm

28. Mary Ann Daniels. Circa 1810.

A charming small sampler embroidered on fine gauze with lustrous floss silks. Worked in satin and cross stitch the sampler is symmetrically composed with twenty small spot motifs. These are mostly comprised of potted plants but also include a pair of birds, a basket of fruit and a small temple-like building.

Framed size: 11" x 11"
28cm x 28cm

Catalogue No 28: Mary Ann Daniels. Circa 1810

29. Louisa Chapman Golding. 1812.

Contained within a colourful honeysuckle and strawberry border this beautifully embroidered sampler has been worked in coloured silks on a cream wool ground.

Genealogical samplers are always interesting and Louisa's sampler gives details of the Chapman Golding family. Contained within a freely worked and decorative floral wreath, tied with blue ribbon, are the birth dates of Louisa's brother John and three sisters, including the death of Elizabeth at the age of six months.

From the dates on the sampler Louisa was twelve years old when she completed her fine sampler.

PROVENANCE. Miss Carrie B Neely. Chicago. Collection. Museum of Science and Industry. Chicago. 1939 - 1998.

Framed size: 17" x 21½"
43cm x 53cm

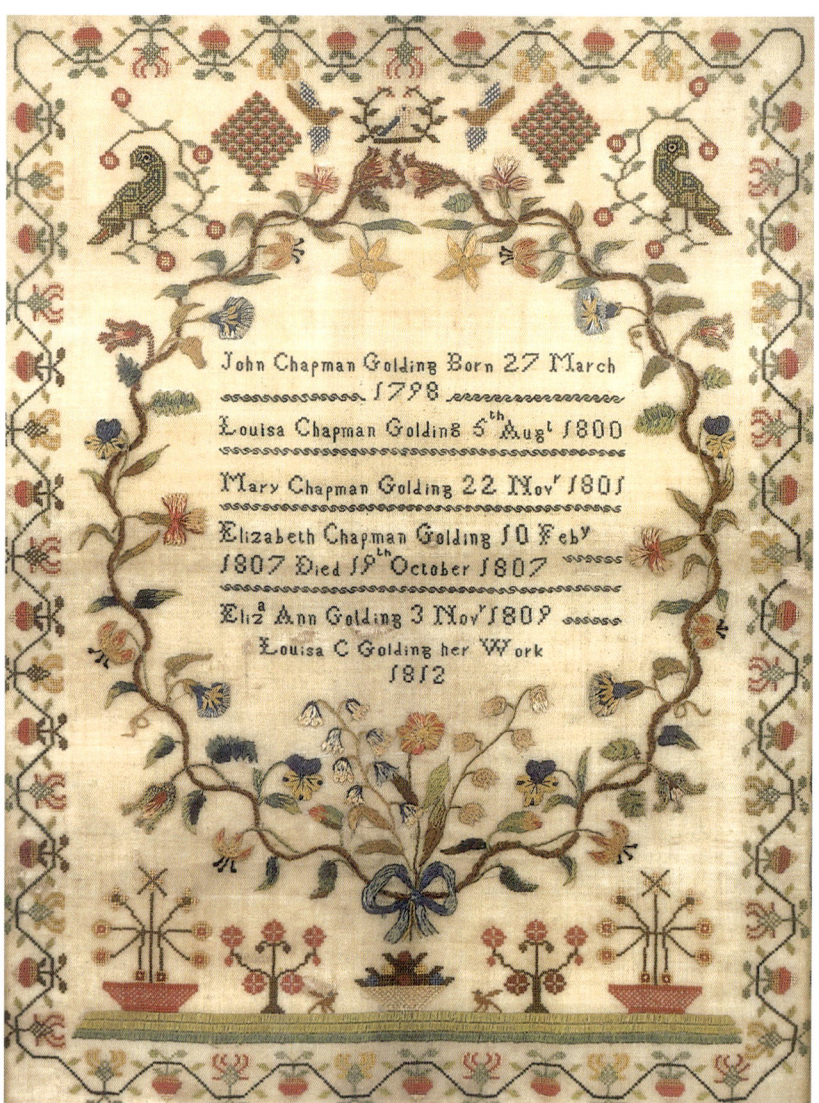

Catalogue No 29: Louisa Chapman Golding. 1812

30. Hannah Leggett. 1813.

Worked in coloured silks on a cream wool ground, Hannah has chosen to mark two great Christian festivals, Christmas Day and Good Friday, by her choice of religious text.

A carnation border forms the surround of the sampler which encloses a number of small motifs which include birds, potted plants, two deer and small crowns. Topiary trees in pots are placed at the bottom of the sampler either side of a large basket of roses.

1813 was the year in which Jane Austen had her novel Pride and Prejudice published. Jane was certainly familiar with the working of samplers and silk embroideries and on a number of occasions makes mention of them in her novels. In Northanger Abbey, Henry Tilney speaking to Catherine Morland says, 'I had entered on my studies at Oxford, while you were a good little girl working your sampler at home!'. In Sense and Sensibility evidence of Charlotte Palmer's expensive education is noted, and that in her bedroom 'there still hung a landscape in coloured silks of her performance in proof of her having spent seven years at a great school in town to some effect.' Again, in Emma, she writes that Mrs Goddard, the owner of a 'real honest old fashioned boarding school' had her parlour 'hung about with fancy work.'*

* Ref: 'Jane Austen's Town and Country Style' Susan Watkins. Pub: Rizolli. New York.

Framed size: 15½" x 18½"
39cm x 47cm

Catalogue No 30: Hannah Leggett. 1813

31. Alice Baker. 1814.

Worked in coloured silks on fine cream wool, this sampler has an immediate pictorial appeal. A large brick, classically proportioned house, with a central panelled door and fan-light above, sits squarely in the bottom half of the sampler, in front of which is a duck pond and a lawn with sheep. Bearing large bunches of fruit, grape vines peep out from either side of the house.

At the top of the sampler an exotic long-tailed bird perches in the branches of a tree whilst outsize butterflies hover over two young women who each play with a dog.

Surrounding the sampler Alice has worked an unusual wide border of roses and rose buds with intertwining stems.

Much use has been made of long and short stitch which produced a rich and lustrous effect and provides texture to the composition.

Catalogue No 31: Alice Baker. 1814

Framed size: 16½" x 21½"
42cm x 55cm

32. Mary Edlow. 1817.

A carefully worked sampler using coloured silks on a fine cream wool ground.

Catalogue No 32: Mary Edlow. 1817.

Numerous pots of flowers are appropriately sprigged around the following six line verse, in which the female virtue of modesty is exalted.

*'Come, my love, and do not spurn
From a little flower learn.
See the lily on the bed
hanging down its modest head;
While it scarcely can be seen,
Folded in its leaf of green.'*

An attractive border of carnations surrounds the sampler, their heads worked in a flat satin stitch.

Framed size: 16½" x 20½"
42cm x 51cm

33. Martha Saxby. 1820.

1820 saw the death of George III and the succession of Prince Regent, George IV. It was also the year in which Florence Nightingale was born and Keat's wrote his poem 'Ode to a Nightingale'.

Appropriately enough, Martha's attractive sampler is scattered with a number of small birds, flowers and animals.

Worked in coloured silks, and with the addition of small glass beads for eyes on some of the images, Martha's sampler shows a high degree of skill in the needle-arts.

Framed size: 25" x 25½"
63cm x 65cm

Catalogue No 33: Martha Saxby. 1820

34. Jane Young. 1822.

This large sampler worked by 10 year old Jane Young on light brown tiffany is particularly complex. Using silks of mainly brown and green shades the young embroideress employs a variety of stitches including cross, long and short, satin and chain.

A large floral design occupies the centre of the sampler, freely worked flowers, leaves and stems are all intertwined and tumble out of a two handled classically shaped urn. Seven smaller panels surround the main motif and consist of a number of rural scenes.

A tribute to Jane's parents is included in the text.

'Behold And / See What My Parents / Has Don For / Me'

Jane Young Daughter of John and Hannah Young Aged 10 Marked This. 'Coatham 1822'.

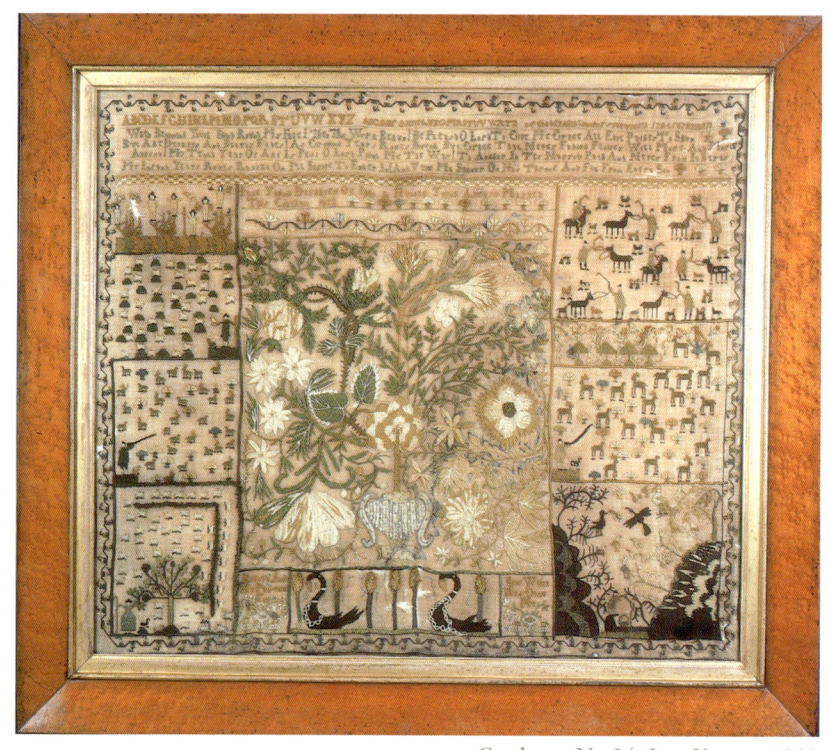

Catalogue No 34: Jane Young. 1822

A long passage of text reads:
'When blooming Youth Shind Round My Face / Then The Work Begun / Be Pleased O Lord To Give Me Grace All Evil Paths To Shun / But Age Decays And Beauty Fades / As Growing Years Rows Round / By Grace Thy Never Fading Flower Will More And More Abound / My Tenth Year Of Age Is Past Oh Lord Point Me The Way To Anchor In Thy Narrow Path And Never From It Stray'.

Framed size: 29" x 33"
74cm x 84cm

35. Louisa Senior. 1823.

This sampler, neatly worked in coloured silks, should be compared with a sampler worked by Harriot Gwyer in 1821, a pupil of Downton School in Hereford. (Illustrated page 30, 'Samplers - Town and Country' published Witney Antiques 1997).

The same source pattern has been used for both samplers, with many almost identical motifs including the pair of young girls with flower baskets and pink dresses, both with skirts decorated with three bands of chevron stripes. A pair of dogs, two large pots of roses, black and white swans, small butterflies etc.

It would appear that Louisa was also a pupil at Downton School and that both girls were taught by the same teacher, possibly following a sampler pattern peculiar to the school.

Framed size: 20" x 21"
51cm x 53cm

Catalogue No 35: Louisa Senior. 1823.

C/F. Sampler by Harriot Gwyer
Downton School. 1821

36. Ann Norden. September the 27th 1826.

Contained within a narrow border worked in cross stitch. The verse positioned below a pot of mixed flowers which includes honeysuckle, rosebuds, lily of the valley, carnation and a single pink tulip.*

The large pictorial motif has been mainly worked with a tambour hook to produce fine chain stitch, the hook picking up loops of thread to form a continuous chain. Many patterns for such tambour work were featured in such periodicals as the 'Lady's Magazine' which was first published in 1770. Tambour work continued in popularity well into the 19th century. The twelve line verse is interesting because Ann has addressed it directly to herself.

'Ann see how your Moment's pafs, How swift they fpeed away....'

Worked in coloured silks on fine wool.

* Four years after this sampler was completed it was recorded that in England the price for a single tulip bulb reached between £100 - £150. Chambers Encyclopaedia. Vol. 13.

Framed size: 15" x 18½"
38cm x 47cm

On the reverse of this sampler:

'At my death this is to go to my nephew Keith Noakes. Signed. B.P.Wright'.

Catalogue No 36: Ann Norden. 1826

37. Ann Marshall. 1826.

This rare memorial sampler was worked just five years after the death of Queen Caroline. (1768 - 1821).
The figure of Britannia leans over a tomb, bearing the inscription 'Sacred to the Memory of Queen Caroline', beneath the branches of a willow tree.

Public sympathy for the Queen, at the hands of her husband George IV, is clearly evident in the sentiments presented in the six lined verse:

'What can atone O ever injured shade
Thy name unhonour'd and thy rites unpaid?
Yet shall thy grave with rising flowers be drest,
And the green turf lie lightly on thy brest
There shall the morn her earliest tears bestow
There the first roses of the year shall blow.'

When George IV came to the throne in 1820 the queen was offered an annuity of £50,000 to renounce her title and live abroad. She refused, and made a triumphal entry into London assuming the rank of royalty and gaining popularity with the public.

The sampler is worked in coloured silks within a honeysuckle border. Baskets of roses and a floral cartouche with a pair of large conifer trees complete the composition.

Framed size: 15" x 19"
38cm x 48cm

Catalogue No 37: Ann Marshall. 1826

38. Charlotte Edlin. 1827.

Catalogue No 38: Charlotte Edlin. 1827

This colourful and minutely stitched sampler is composed of a myriad of flowers, small birds, insects and figures, filling every inch of the fine cream woollen ground upon which it has been worked.

Cross, chain, petit point and satin stitch have been used to create this truly remarkable piece of childhood embroidery and it is difficult to conceive that this highly accomplished embroideress was only ten years old.

The inclusion of a small figure of a livered black boy is interesting and although slavery was abolished in England in 1807, motifs of this type were still being used on samplers. The Emancipation Act banning slavery in the British Empire did not occur however, until 1833.

The popular verse found on a number of samplers provides four lines of text.

FRIENDSHIP

'Tell me, ye knowing and discerning few,
Where I may find a Friend both firm and true,
Who dares stand by me when in deep Distress
And then his Love and Friendship most express'

Loan Exhibit.

Framed Size: 18" x 13½"
45cm x 33cm

39. Mary Robertson. Circa 1830.

A fine embroidered sampler worked on a cream wool ground in fine silks, the colours being predominantly green, pink, brown and beige. Enclosed within an undulating, geometric floral border with a central verse.

Many samplers dating from the years 1830 - 1840 use a colour palette of greens and browns with a slight relief of pink or blue. Many also follow a familiar form, using a short centrally positioned moralistic verse, geometric flower border and numerous small bowls of potted plants.
The samplers by Ellen Lucas, Mary Robertson and Mary Jarrard are such good examples of samplers from this period which follow this pattern.

PROVENANCE. Miss Carrie B Neely. Chicago. Collection. Museum of Science and Industry. Chicago. 1939 - 1998.

Framed size: 17" x 18"
43cm x 46cm

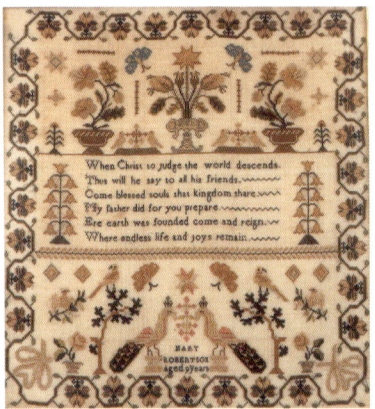

Catalogue No 39: Mary Robertson. Circa 1830.

Catalogue No 40: Ellen Lucas. Age 12. 1835

40. Ellen Lucas. Age 12. May 2 1835.

Contained within an undulating floral border this perfectly symmetrical sampler has a strong visual appeal. Designed with numerous pots and baskets of flowering plants, it fits perfectly into our exhibition theme.

The chosen text is particularly appropriate and is one rarely found on a sampler.

*'We should
From works of nature
Gather a teacher
And all to seek
The paths of peace
And glorify our maker'*

Worked in coloured silks on fine wool.

Framed size: 16½" x 20½"
42cm x 52cm

41. Mary Jarrard. 1837.

At the age of thirteen, Mary Jarrard embroidered her attractive sampler as a memorial to her father.

*'For the lofs of my father I mourn
My kind an affectionate friend
To Jesus I hope he is gone
To heaven I hope he ll ascend.'*

Worked in silks on fine wool, this well balanced sampler is contained within a narrow honeysuckle border and is sprigged with attractive motifs which include birds, animals, flowers and potted plants.

The initials LVS embroidered below the name and date, may stand for Licensed Victuallers School, a charitable educational establishment founded by the Licensed Victuallers Society in 1803.

Basic education was provided, and in common with many charity schools, needlework figured prominently for the girls on the school's curriculum. Shirts, sheets, shifts, tableware etc was produced for sale which provided an income to help in the financing of the school.

Some of the early records of the school no longer exist so we have been unable to find any record of Mary.

Catalogue No 41: Mary Jarrard. 1837

Ref. 'Licensed Victuallers School. 1803 - 1978'.
D.J.K.Walters.M.A.

Framed size: 18½" x 16"
47cm x 40cm

Catalogue No 42: M.A.Cartwright. 1837

42. M.A.Cartwright. 1837.

Sampler worked in coloured silks on fine wool by nine year old M.A.Cartwright. A beautiful and freely worked meandering border of mixed flowers including tulips, a peony, carnations and rosebuds etc, frames the top and sides of the sampler.
The central area contains rows of border patterns, alphabets and numerals and the popular sampler verse beginning:
'Next unto God, dear Parents I address,
Myself to you in Humble Thankfulness.....'

The influence and increased popularity of Berlin pattern books is clearly shown in the realistic and carefully charted cross stitch embroidery of the church set in a country landscape which has been placed towards the bottom of the sampler.

Framed size: 20½" x 18"
51cm x 45cm

Catalogue No 43: Ann Sheppard. 1844

43. Ann Sheppard. 1844.

This very unusual and extremely striking embroidery employs two distinctly different techniques.

Worked on a silk ground the embroidery depicts Christ and the woman of Samaria, together at the well. Worked in spectacularly vibrant coloured silks, the two figures have their faces painted directly onto the background silk. This combination of painting and silk embroidery was fashionable during the late 18th century and early 19th century.

In a large oval cartouche in the top section, Ann has embroidered her name, her age as being eleven years, and the date in small metallic beads.

Surrounding the composition is a complicated floral border worked in Berlin wools. This supplies a contrast to the silk work which may possibly have been started some years earlier and finished by Ann in 1844.

Framed size: 23" x 24½"
58cm x 62cm

44. S.H. 1846.

An exceptionally finely worked two part sampler on fine muslin or tiffany, the cross stitch used on such a fine scale as to allow great detail.

The pictorial top section is perfectly symmetrical with tiny spot motifs, which include a pair of cherubs holding 'the crown of life', baskets of fruit, small animals and birds, fruiting vines, a large bowl of carnations and sprays of roses. The word 'Gratitude' appears twice placed below a pair of star motifs.

The second sampler contains a long religious verse on the subject of life and death.

'When rising from the bed of death, O'er whelm'd with guilt and fear.....'

The fineness of the stitching has much in common with work produced in some orphanages and asylums in England during the 19th century. Although no such name has been recorded on the sampler, it is quite probable that this piece is another example.

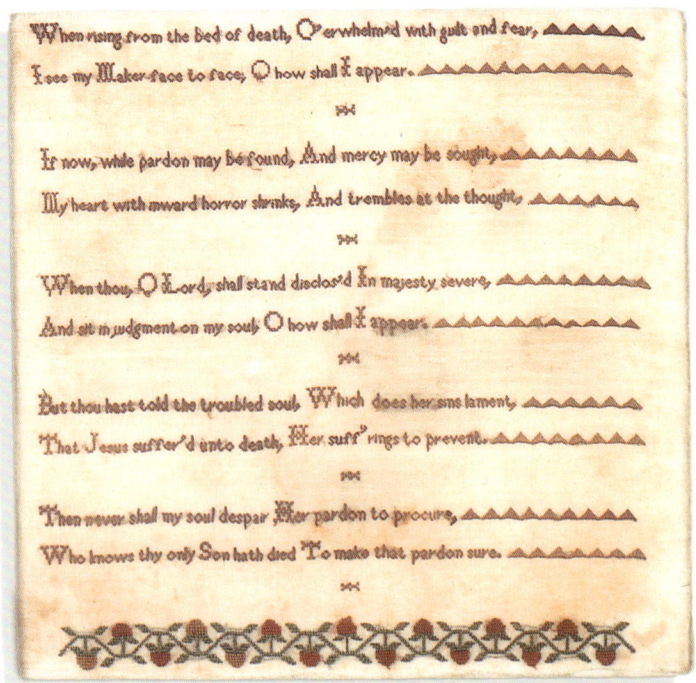

Probably intended to make up into a bag or small cushion.

Catalogue No 44: S.H. 1846

Framed size: 12" x 21"
31cm x 53cm

45. Alice Rowland. June 10th 1857.

A plain marking sampler worked in red cotton on linen. Rows of alphabets, numerals and narrow border patterns occupy the top half of the sampler, and a short two verse poem 'To the Crocus' the bottom. These particular verses fit perfectly into the theme of the exhibition and have not been encountered before on a sampler by ourselves.

'To the Crocus
Lowly, sprightly little flower:
Herald of a brighter bloom,
Bursting in a sunny hour
From thy winter tomb.

Hues you bring, bright, gay, and tender,
As if never to decay;
Fleeting in their varied splendour.
Soon, alas! it fades away'.

Framed size: 15½" x 17"
39cm x 43cm

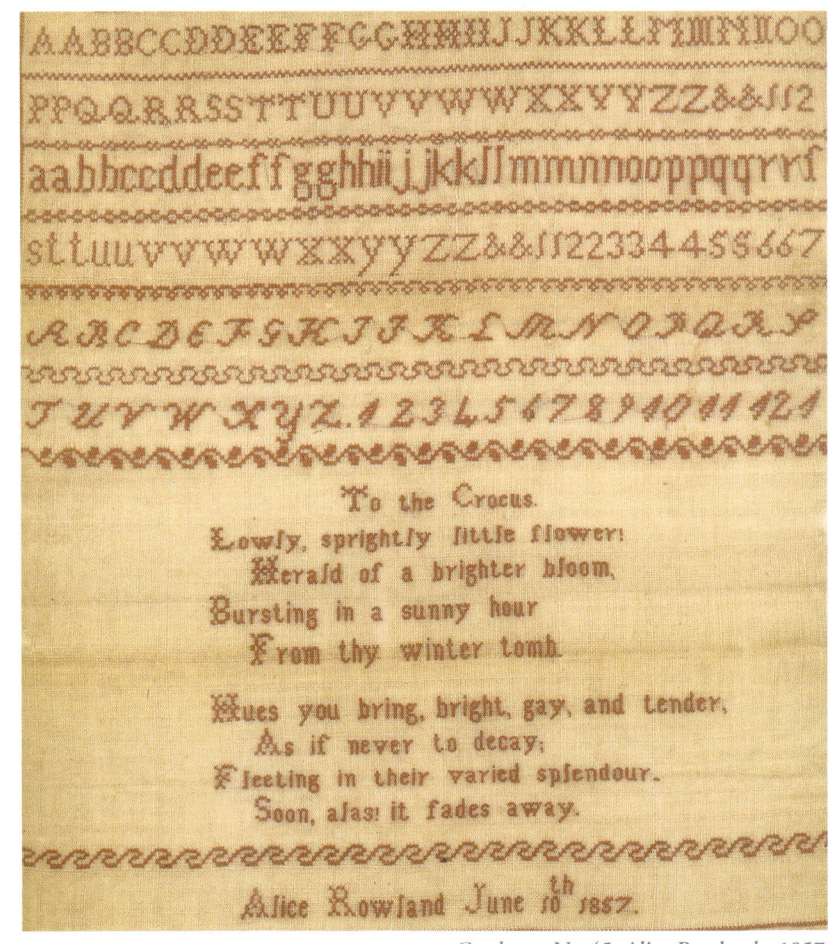

Catalogue No 45: Alice Rowland. 1857

Witney Antiques Textile Collection.

At our showrooms in Witney we probably hold the largest stock of antique needlework samplers for sale in the country.
With between sixty and one hundred samplers always on display a visit is always worthwhile. This stock may be viewed at any time in our specialist department and also during the period of this special exhibition.
We also stock 17th century raised and silk work textiles and 18th century silk pictures.

Since this catalogue went to press we have acquired other samplers which will be included in the exhibition.

Catalogues Available by Post from Witney Antiques.

An 'A - Z of British 18th and 19th Century Samplers'
A general collection of antique needlework samplers.

Samplers. 'A School Room Exercise'
A collection of antique needlework samplers recording the school, institution or teacher under whose instruction the sampler was made.

Samplers. 'House and Garden'
A collection of antique needlework samplers depicting the British house and garden.

Samplers. 'All Creatures Great And Small'
A collection of antique samplers themed around animals, birds and insects.

Samplers. 'Town and Country'
A collection of antique samplers naming the towns and villages in which they were worked.
Including a collection of rare map samplers.

Samplers and Historic Embroideries. 'How Fragrant the Rose'. 1660 - 1860.